The Europe Project Book

CONTENTS

Europe	2	Luxembourg	18
Belgium	4	The Netherlands	20
Denmark	6	Portugal	22
France	8	Spain	24
Germany	10	United Kingdom	26
Greece	12	Neighbours	28
Republic of Ireland	14	Quick Quiz	30
Italy	16	Answers to Quick Quiz	32

Audrey Daly • Illustrated by Andrew Warrington

Headway · Hodder & Stoughton

CW00970748

EUROPE

What is Europe?

The continent of Europe is the world's second smallest continent. It is made up of many countries.

What is the European Community?

Twelve of the countries of Europe have joined together to form the European Community. This means the countries can work together and help one another. The European Community will be a much stronger power in the world than any of the countries could be on their own.

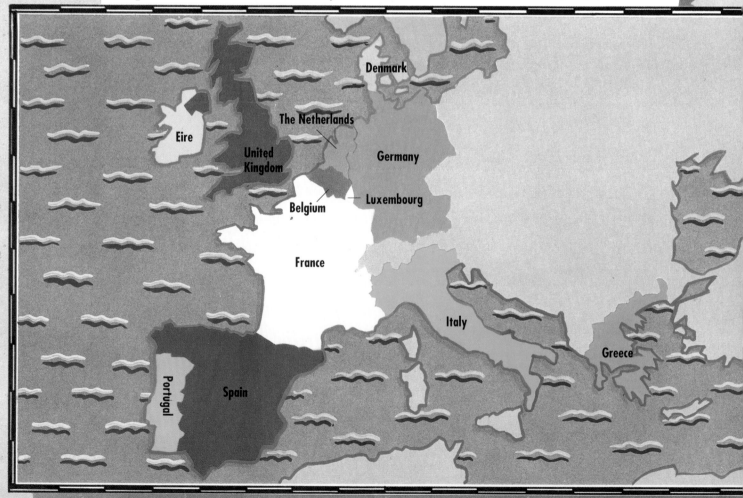

How the European Community started

1952 Belgium, France, Italy, West Germany and the Netherlands banded together to control their coal and steel industries.

1957 These six nations formed the European Economic Community (EEC) under the Treaty of Rome.

1973 Britain, Denmark and the Republic of Ireland joined the EEC.

1981 Greece joined.

1985 Portugal and Spain joined, to make twelve members in all, including East Germany, which became part of the EC on 3 October 1990 when it was reunited with West Germany.

1992 The Single European Market was established. Special laws now make it easier to work and trade with other countries in the EC.

How it works

European Commission

There are seventeen Commissioners. Larger countries send two and smaller countries one. The Commission suggests new laws for the Community, and plans how the Community money is spent.

European Parliament

There are 518 Members of the European Parliament (MEPs). Larger countries have more MEPs than smaller countries. The Parliament discusses the proposals of the Commission, and decides whether they should go ahead .

Council of Ministers

This group is made up of one Minister from each country. They make decisions on major issues for the Community.

European Court of Justice

The European Court of Justice is made up of thirteen judges. They hear cases involving Community law.

European Council

Heads of government attend the European Council. They meet to discuss how the countries can co-operate better.

BELGIUM

FACT FILE

Population 9,858,895.

Area 30,513 square kilometres.

Terrain Very flat – its largest hill is only 694 metres high.

Capital city Brussels.

Currency Belgian franc (BF) of 100 centimes.

BRUSSELS ·

Language French and Dutch are both official languages. Flemish is also spoken.

Exports Chocolates and pâté. Belgian chocolates are famous world-wide, and there are shops in Belgium which sell only chocolates.

Schools Children can go to school as young as 2 years old, and stay until they are 18. Belgium is one of the few countries where everyone can read and write.

Wildlife Boars, wildcats, and deer.

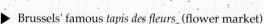

▶ Brussels' famous *tapis des fleurs* (flower market)

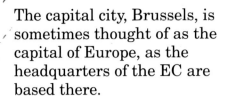

The capital city, Brussels, is sometimes thought of as the capital of Europe, as the headquarters of the EC are based there.

Cycling is a favourite sport because the country is so flat. The Tour de France has been won by a Belgian on several occasions.

René Magritte (1898–1967) was a famous Belgian artist. He painted very strange pictures, which had everyday objects like apples and bowler hats in odd situations.

Now you see!

Can you match these European countries with their shapes?

Luxembourg   France
Germany   Spain

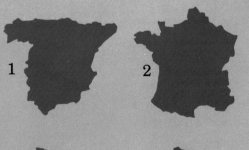

1   2
3   4

Did you know?

Since both Dutch and French are spoken in Belgium, street signs have to be written in 2 languages, so that everyone can understand them.

▼ Greenland

DENMARK

FACT FILE

Population 5,130,000.

Area 43,069 square kilometres.

Terrain Mostly flat, with some gently rolling hills, the highest of which is only 173 metres.

Capital city Copenhagen.

Currency Danish krone (Kr) of 100 øre.

Language Danish (similar to Swedish and Norwegian).

Famous exports Bacon, butter and other farming produce, furniture.

Schools Children must attend school from the age of 7 to 16. Daycare centres for younger children are run by the state.

Wildlife Red deer, foxes and hares.

COPENHAGEN •

DANMARK 4.75

DANMARK 4.75

Danepak

Denmark is made up of the Jutland Peninsula, which joins on to Germany, and about 500 islands. Most of the islands are small, but one of them, Greenland, is the largest island in the world.

Greenland has an area of 2,175,600 square kilometres, and lies near the North Pole many miles from Denmark. The people who live there are mainly Inuits. Although it is part of Denmark, it has its own Prime Minister and does not belong to the European Community.

Not long ago, the body of a man, now called the Tollund Man, was found in the bogs of northern Denmark. He had been there over 2,000 years, but his stomach contained the remains of his last meal – porridge.

▲ The Tollund Man

The famous Lego building bricks are made in Denmark. Legoland is an amazing theme park where everything is made from Lego.

▼ The statue of the little mermaid, a character from a fairy tale by Danish author Hans Christian Andersen, watches over the port of Copenhagen

Did you know?

The word lego comes from two Danish words, *leg godt*, which mean 'play well'.

Now you see!

Which countries do these newspapers come from?

EL PAIS

Le Monde

DIE WELT

LA STAMPA

FRANCE

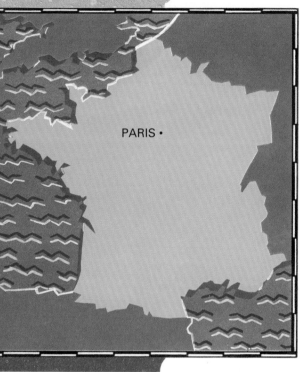

PARIS •

FACT FILE

Population 55,873,000.

Area 547,026 square kilometres including the island of Corsica where Napoleon was born. France is the largest country in the European Community.

Terrain Snow-capped mountains, beautiful beaches and farmland.

Capital city Paris.

Currency French franc (F) of 100 centimes.

Language French – but Alsatian, Flemish, Breton and Basque dialects are still spoken in parts of France.

Famous exports Wines, perfume, cheeses, pottery, wool and fashion. France produces a third of the world's wine.

Schools Children in France go to school from the age of 6 to 16. School usually starts at 8 or 8.30 a.m. and can go on until 5 or 6 p.m. French children have lessons on Saturday mornings as well, although they get Wednesday afternoons off.

Wildlife Foxes, squirrels, bears, wildcats and mountain deer (chamois) are all found in France. In one region of France, the Camargue, there are wild horses.

▼ Wild h

French people love races of all kinds, including horse races, cycle races, car races and even the Beaujolais Nouveau wine race!

The **Tour de France** is the world famous cycle race. The cyclists race all around the country – a route of 4,800 kilometres.

The **Le Mans 24 hour race** is a tough car race where the cars race day and night round the streets of the town of Le Mans.

Art has always been popular in France. The cave paintings of Lascaux are of buffaloes, horses and red deer, and were painted about 13,000 BC.

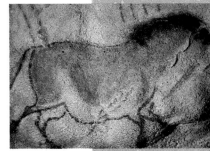

A famous place for artists in Paris today is the Place du Tertre.

Now you see!

Four of these famous landmarks are in Europe. Can you match them to their capital cities? The fifth is a long way away!

1

2

3

4   5

Did you know?

The Eiffel Tower is over a hundred years old. It is 320.75 metres to the top of its television aerial.

in the Camargue

GERMANY

FACT FILE

Population 78,673,632.

Area 356,755 square kilometres.

Terrain Large rivers, lakes, moors, hills and mountains.

Capital city Berlin.

Currency Deutsche Mark (DM) of 100 pfennig.

Language German.

Exports Cars, wines, cameras, binoculars and other optical instruments

Schools Children in Germany must go to school from 6 to 15 years old. School starts at 8 a.m. and finishes at 1 p.m. In the afternoon there is no school.

Wildlife Chamois and ibex can be seen in the Alpine regions, as well as golden eagles. Other wildlife includes wild boar, hares, wildcats, lynx, beavers and badgers.

BERLIN ·

Germany is one of the greatest industrial nations, and is the richest country in Europe.

A German engineer, Karl Benz, built the first car to be made commercially. He built the first petrol-driven car in 1885. Today, German cars, like BMW, Volkswagen and Mercedes-Benz, are famous all over the world.

The Rhine is one of the biggest German rivers. There are many vineyards along its valley.

The Lorelei is a rock on the Rhine which has an amazing echo, which some people mistake for a song.

East and West Germany were divided after the Second World War. There were great celebrations in 1990 when the Berlin Wall was pulled down and people travelled long distances to attend the party.

East and West Germany were officially reunited later that year, in October.

Now you see!

Can you match the numbered countries with their names?

Spain   France   Belgium   UK
Germany   Eire   Portugal   Luxembourg

1.   2.   3.   4.

5.   6.   7.   8.

Did you know?

There are currently no speed limits on German motorways so cars can travel very fast.

GREECE

FACT FILE

Population 10,013,000.

Area 131,944 square kilometres. About one tenth of Greece's area is made up of islands.

Terrain Mountainous country surrounded on three sides by sea. Its jagged coastline is 14,480 kilometres long.

Capital city Athens.

Currency Drachma (Dr) of 100 leptae.

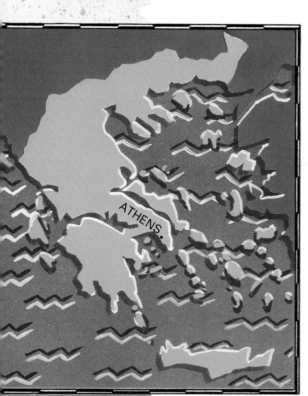

Language Modern Greek.

Exports Currants (Great Britain buys most of them), sponges, olive oil. Fresh fruit and vegetables are becoming an important export.

Schools Children must attend school from the age of 6 to 15.

Wildlife In the forests there are roe deer, wildcats, wild boar, lynxes, wolves and brown bears. In the Mediterranean areas there are jackals, wild goats and porcupines.

▲ Mount Oly

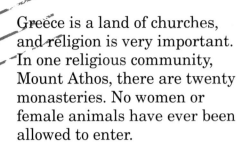

Greece is a land of churches, and religion is very important. In one religious community, Mount Athos, there are twenty monasteries. No women or female animals have ever been allowed to enter.

Mount Olympus in Greece was the home of the legendary Greek gods and goddesses, such as Zeus, Athena and Apollo.

The first Olympic Games were held at Olympia in Greece in 776 BC. Women were not allowed to be present at the games and the male contestants were naked. The modern Olympic Games are now very different. They have been held every four years since 1896, and are the most important international sporting competition.

Greece is popular with tourists. It is visited for its beaches and historical sites. The Ancient Greeks were very clever, and created beautiful buildings and sculptures. Many of the ruins of the buildings can still be seen today.

Did you know?

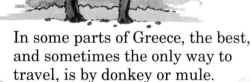

In some parts of Greece, the best, and sometimes the only way to travel, is by donkey or mule.

Now you see!

The Modern Greek alphabet looks very different from the one most European languages use. Compare the letters below with their equivalent sounds in the Roman alphabet.

α β γ δ ε ζ η θ ι κ λ μ ν ξ ο π ρ σ τ υ φ χ ψ ω

a b g d ĕ z ē th i k l m n x ŏ p r s t y ph k ps ō

Write your name using Greek letters – or send a secret message to a friend!

REPUBLIC OF IRELAND
(ALSO CALLED EIRE)

FACT FILE

Population 3,535,000.

Area 70,283 square kilometres.

Terrain Flat in the centre, with mountains in a ring round the coast.

Capital city Dublin.

Currency Punt (Irish pound – IR£) of 100 pence.

Language Irish – English is the second official language.

Famous exports Linens, laces and fine glassware.

Schools Children must attend school from the age of 6 to 14 years old.

Wildlife Red deer are protected in the Kerry Mountains, and hedgehogs, shrews, hares and badgers can be seen in other parts of Ireland.

DUBLIN •

▲ An Irish

◄ A Celtic cross

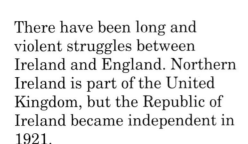

There have been long and violent struggles between Ireland and England. Northern Ireland is part of the United Kingdom, but the Republic of Ireland became independent in 1921.

In Ireland, part of the land is peat bog. Peat is formed when dead leaves and plants rot. It is used as fuel in both homes and industry.

Ireland is known as the Emerald Isle, because of its lush green countryside. Cows graze in the fields and produce milk, butter and cream.

The national badge of Ireland is the shamrock.

DUBLIN

echaun

Now you see!

Can you name the breeds of dogs below and say which countries they come from traditionally?

1

2

Did you know?

3

4

In Ireland there are no snakes at all. There is a legend that when St Patrick (the patron saint of Ireland) was clearing out all the vermin from the country in the fifth century AD, the very last serpent didn't want to leave. He lured it into a small box, slammed the lid and threw the box into the sea.

◀ Linen making

ITALY

FACT FILE

The Tarantella (a traditional dance)

Population 57,441,000.

Area 301,225 square kilometres, including the islands of Sardinia, Elba, Ischia, Sicily, Capri and about 70 other islands.

Terrain Mostly mountainous, with two fertile coastal plains.

Capital city Rome.

Currency Lira (L) of 100 centesimi.

Language Italian.

Famous exports Cars, leather goods, textiles, sulphur (found in Sicily).

Schools Children must go to school from 6 to 14 years old, and their education is free.

Wildlife There is a great deal of wildlife to be found in the mountains – marmots, ermine, mountain partridge, ibex, chamois, roe deer, brown bears, lynx, stoats, foxes and wolves.

The island of Sardinia has mouflon sheep, fallow deer and wild boar.

Sharks and swordfish are found in the seas round southern Italy.

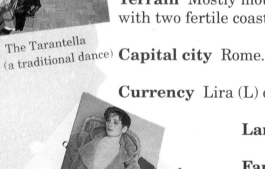

• ROME

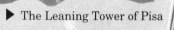
▶ The Leaning Tower of Pisa

Italy is made up of a long thin mainland country, which many people think looks like a boot, and many islands, including Sicily and Sardinia. Some of the smaller islands are uninhabited, and some are used as prisons.

Mount Etna in Sicily is a live volcano which last erupted in 1985. It is the highest volcano in Europe. Even though it is still very much alive, people grow oranges on its slopes because the soil is so good.

Another Italian volcano is Mount Vesuvius. When it erupted in AD 79, the town of Pompeii (just 1.6 kilometres away) was buried under cinders, small stones and ashes! Today you can walk through its ruins which have been excavated.

▲ Pompeii

▲ Vesuvius

Did you know?

In Venice, which is built on islands in a lagoon, there are canals instead of roads. Gondolas and small boats take the place of taxis, cars and buses.

▲ Venice

Now you see!

Can you recognise these countries in their own languages?

Deutschland

Italia

Nederland

Belgique

Österreich

Cymru

Spaghetti is a favourite Italian food, which can be messy to eat. To eat it properly twirl it round a fork, but don't cut it – this is considered unlucky!

LUXEMBOURG

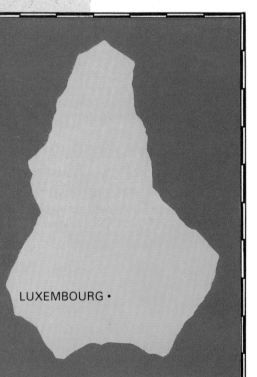

LUXEMBOURG •

FACT FILE

Population 378,400.

Area 2,586 square kilometres.

Terrain A high-level land cut by deep river valleys with forests on the hillsides.

Capital city Luxembourg, where the Court of Justice of the European Community is situated.

Currency Luxembourg franc (LF) of 100 centimes (equal to one Belgian franc). Belgian currency is also legal tender.

Language French is the official language, but Letzeburgesch (or Luxembourgois) is spoken too. Most people also speak German.

Exports Iron and steel products.

Schools Most children go to school until they are 19 although the school leaving age is 13.

Wildlife Deer, wild boar.

◀ Much of Luxembourg is covered with beautiful pine forests

Luxembourg is a small country surrounded by Belgium, Germany and France.

Luxembourg is a well-known broadcasting centre. Radio Luxembourg broadcasts in English and can be listened to throughout Europe. It plays pop music.

The traditional dancing procession at Echternach takes place every year.

▶ The Echternach dancing procession

Now you see!

Most countries have one or more particular foods they are known for. Can you match these to their countries?

 Snails

Pastries

 Spaghetti

Paella

Frankfurters

LUXEMBOURG

The city of Luxembourg is home to the European Community Court and also the Secretariat of the European Parliament.

Luxembourg was once a fortress, and its name is believed to come from the Celtic word *lucilinburhuc* meaning 'little castle'.

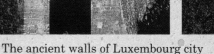

▲ The ancient walls of Luxembourg city

THE NETHERLANDS

FACT FILE

Population 14,891,000.

Area 40,844 square kilometres.

Terrain A low, flat land, crossed by canals and rivers.

Capital city Amsterdam.

Currency Dutch guilder or florin (fl) of 100 cents.

Language Dutch.

Exports Tulips, Edam and Gouda cheeses.

Schools Dutch children must attend school from 6 to 14 years of age.

Wildlife Although badgers and hawks have disappeared from the countryside, the boar has been introduced and red grouse are protected.

• AMSTERDAM

75c 40 JAAR NAVO NEDERLAN

KLAROP Zoute drop
KLAROP Zoute drop
Droste HOLLAND Pastilles

Over a quarter of the Netherlands is below sea level. Some land, called *polderland*, has been reclaimed from the sea. Dykes have been built to keep the sea out.

Rotterdam is the largest port in the world. Raw materials are imported for the Dutch industries.

The Netherlands exports more tulips than any other country in the world.

Everyone in the Netherlands rides a bicycle, because the land is so flat. There are special bicycle lanes everywhere.

Ice-skating is a popular sport in the Netherlands. The *Elfstedentocht* (Eleven Towns Race) is a skating race over 190 kilometres of frozen canals.

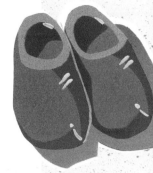

Now you see!

Some countries are famous for particular cars. Which countries make these?

Volkswagen

Citroën 2CV

Mini

Fiat

Did you know?

The Dutch are very neat and clean – perhaps because their land is so crowded. There are more people per square kilometre in the Netherlands than in almost any other country in the world.

PORTUGAL

FACT FILE

Population 10,408,000 including the Azores and Madeira.

Area 92,082 square kilometres including the Azores and Madeira.

Terrain A land of mountains, plains and rivers.

Capital city Lisbon.

Currency Escudo (Esc) of 100 centavos.

There are many beautiful golf courses in Portugal

Language Portuguese.

Famous exports Sardines and anchovies, port and Madeira wine, and cork.

Schools Children have to attend school from the age of 6 to the age of 15.

Wildlife Wild goats, wild pigs, deer, wolves, lynx, foxes and Iberian hares are all found in the mountains.

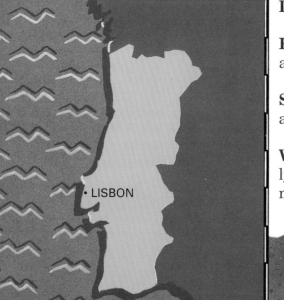

• LISBON

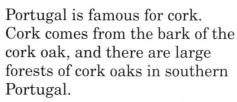

The Portuguese have always been great sailors, and Portugal used to have a huge empire. A Portuguese ship captained by Ferdinand Magellan first went round the world, and at one time the royal Portuguese capital was Rio de Janeiro in Brazil.

Although Portugal no longer has an Empire, Portuguese is still spoken in parts of South America, Africa and the Far East.

Portugal is famous for cork. Cork comes from the bark of the cork oak, and there are large forests of cork oaks in southern Portugal.

There are bullfights in Portugal, but unlike in other countries the bull doesn't get killed.

▲ Magellan's ship

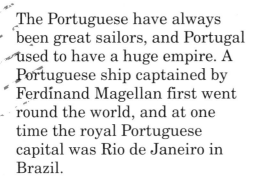

Now you hear!

The Portuguese say 'sim' for 'yes' and 'não' for 'no'. Here are some more words that mean 'yes' and 'no' in foreign languages. Can you match these words to the countries they come from?

ja, nein   France

oui, non   The Netherlands

si, no   Germany

ja, neen   Spain or Italy

Did you know?

Portugal and England have been allies since the Treaty of Windsor was signed in 1386.

SPAIN

FACT FILE

Population 39,054,000.

Area 504,782 square kilometres.

Terrain A high flat land surrounded by mountains.

Capital city Madrid.

Currency Peseta (Pta) of 100 centimos.

Language Spanish.

MADRID •

A flamenco dancer ▼

Exports Oranges, cork, olive oil, wines including sherry, iron ore, mercury.

Schools Children must go to school from the age of 6 until they are 14.

Wildlife There are bears and wolves in the Pyrenees and northern mountains. Spanish ibex, deer and wild pigs are kept in reserves to protect them.

◀ Seafood paella

ESPAÑA

In Madrid is the statue of one of Spain's most famous authors Miguel de Cervantes, who wrote *Don Quixote*. This is the story of a knight and his servant who have many adventures. The knight's mind is over-imaginative, and leads him to think objects are enemies. In one story he has a fight with a windmill!

The Flamenco is a lively Spanish dance. The music is played on guitars and castanets, and the women often wear bright, frilly dresses.

Many people go on holiday to Spain for its sun, sand, sea and good food. Each year there are about 50,000 visitors, mainly staying in seaside resorts.

Now you see!

All the European Community countries enjoy football, but some have special games. Can you match these games with their countries?

Eire

Cricket   Boules

Spain

Jai Alai
                          UK
France

Hurling

Did you know?

A special breed of savage bull is used in Spanish bullfights. At the end of a really exciting fight, the matador receives both ears and the tail. Matadors are usually very rich as well as famous.

UNITED KINGDOM

LONDON •

FACT FILE

Population 55,848,000.

Area 244,098.8 square kilometres.

Terrain Varied landscape with hills and mountains, fenland and lakes.

Currency Pound sterling (£) of 100 new pence.

▲ The Houses of Parliament, London

Language English.

Exports Cars, oil, chemicals, industrial plant.

Schools Children must go to school from 5 to 16 years of age.

Wildlife Deer, badgers, otters, foxes, squirrels and brown hares (mountain hares in Scotland). There is one poisonous snake (the adder) and two other non-poisonous ones.

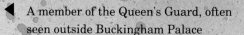

◀ A member of the Queen's Guard, often seen outside Buckingham Palace

The United Kingdom is made up of the island of Great Britain, the north-eastern part of Ireland and over 400 smaller islands. Many of the small islands, like the Farne Islands in Northumberland, are inhabited only by birds and seals.

Ben Nevis in Scotland is the highest mountain in the United Kingdom. It rises to 1,343 metres, with a cairn on top of 3.65 metres. The second highest mountain is Snowdon in Wales. This has a railway going right to the top.

In Wales some people speak Welsh. All road signs are written in Welsh and English.

The only major tennis tournament to be played on grass is at Wimbledon in London. The tournament was first played in 1877. Although tennis is popular, cricket is considered to be the national game. Football and rugby are also popular.

CYMRU WALES

▲ A cricket match

Now you see!

Can you tell which countries these cars come from?

E GR D

I

GB

DK

Did you know?

The United Kingdom is one of the few places in the world where milk is delivered to the door. And milk is still sold in the United Kingdom by the pint, even though most other measurements are now metric.

◀ Morris dancing

NEIGHBOURS

Some of the countries in Europe are not yet part of the European Community, although they may join later. Five countries have already applied to join: Austria, Cyprus, Malta, Turkey and Sweden.

Albania

Population 3,410,000.

Area 28,748 square kilometres.

Capital Tirana.

Bulgaria

Population 8,995,000.

Area 110,912 square kilometres.

Capital Sofia.

Roses are one of Bulgaria's main crops.

Monaco

Population 27,063.

Area 195 hectares.

Capital Monaco-Ville.

▲ Monaco-Ville harbour

If the ruler of Monaco ever dies without an heir or heiress, the state will become a self-governing French protectorate.

Austria

Population 7,595,000.

Area 83,849 square kilometres.

Capital Vienna.

▲ Vienna

Vienna is an international centre for music and musicians.

Czechoslovakia

Population 15,608,000.

Area 127,869 square kilometres.

Capital Prague.

The famous Bohemian glass is made in Czechoslovakia.

Poland

Population 37,862,000.

Area 312,677 square kilometres.

Capital Warsaw.

Poland is one of the greatest coal-producing countries in Europe.

Sweden

Population 8,462,000.

Area 449,964 square kilometres.

Capital Stockholm.

▲ Stockholm

Sweden is the biggest of the Scandinavian states.

Switzerland

Population 6,620,000.

Area 41,293 square kilometres.

Capital Berne.

Swiss watches are known throughout the world.

Turkey

Population 52,422,000.

Area 780,576 square kilometres.

Capital Ankara.

You must always be polite in Turkey. If you insult anyone, you get thrown in jail!

Yugoslavia

▲ Istanbul, Turkey

Population 23,559,000.

Area 255,804 square kilometres.

Capital Belgrade.

Yugoslavia has become a popular place for holidays.

QUICK QUIZ

1 Which volcano has orange groves on its slopes?

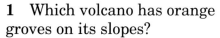

2 What is the currency used in Portugal?

3 Where is the world's major lawn tennis championship held?

4 Which is the largest island in the world?

5 In which country can everyone read and write?

6 What mustn't you do in Turkey?

7 How many MEPs are there?

8 What is the capital of Luxembourg?

9 Who built the first car to be made commercially?

10 What is the Irish pound called?

11 Which is the highest mountain in the United Kingdom?

12 What is *polderland,* and where is it found?

13 Where do they use boats instead of taxis?

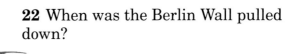

22 When was the Berlin Wall pulled down?

23 What are found in the Camargue area of France?

14 In which country are there no snakes?

24 Which people like ice-skating?

15 Where did the artist René Magritte come from?

25 Where is Legoland?

16 Which country exports tulips?

26 How old is the Eiffel Tower in Paris?

17 Where is the European Court of Justice?

18 What is the main difference between Portuguese and Spanish bullfights?

19 Which countries have applied to join the European Community?

20 What is the school leaving age in the United Kingdom?

21 Where were the first Olympic games held?

27 Which city is an international centre for music?

28 How long does it take peat to form?

29 When did Britain join the European Community?

Answers to Quick Quiz

1 Mount Etna in Sicily
2 The escudo
3 Wimbledon, London
4 Greenland
5 Belgium
6 Insult people
7 518
8 Luxembourg
9 The German engineer Karl Marx
10 The punt
11 Ben Nevis
12 Land reclaimed from the sea in the Netherlands
13 Venice in Italy
14 Ireland
15 Belgium
16 The Netherlands
17 Luxembourg
18 The bull doesn't get killed in Portugal
19 Austria, Cyprus, Malta, Sweden and Turkey
20 16
21 Olympia, Greece
22 1990
23 Wild horses
24 The Dutch in the Netherlands
25 Denmark
26 Over 100 years old
27 Vienna in Austria
28 Ten years
29 1973

Answers to Now you see!

page 5 1 Spain 2 France 3 Germany
4 Luxembourg
page 7 El País - Spain; Die Welt - Germany; Le Monde - France; La Stampa - Italy.
page 9 1 Arc de Triomphe - Paris; 2 Colosseum - Rome; 3 Taj Mahal - Agra, India; 4 Nelson's Column - London; 5 Parthenon - Athens.
page 11 1 UK 2 Eire 3 Belgium 4 Germany
5 Spain 6 Luxembourg 7 Portugal 8 France.
page 15 1 Dachshund - Germany; 2 Wolfhound - Eire; 3 Cocker Spaniel - Spain; 4 Poodle - France.
page 17 Nederland - The Netherlands; Cymru - Wales; Belgique - Belgium; Deutschland - Germany; Italia - Italy, Österreich - Austria
page 19 Paella - Spain; spaghetti- Italy; snails - France; pastries - Denmark; frankfurters - Germany.
page 21 Volkswagen - Germany; 2CV - France; Mini - UK; Fiat - Italy.
page 23 ja, nein - Germany; oui, non - France; si, no - Spain or Italy; ja, neen - The Netherlands.
page 25 Jai alai - Spain; hurling - Eire; cricket - UK; boules - France.
page 27 E - Spain; GR - Greece; D - Germany; I - Italy; GB - United Kingdom, DK - Denmark.

Acknowledgements

The author and publishers would like to thank the following for permission to reproduce photographic material in this book: Associated Press p11t; Austrian National Tourist Office p28br; BMW (GB) Limited/Park Avenue Productions p21b; Bridgeman Art Gallery, London/The Son of Man, 1964, Rene Magritte, © ADAGP, Paris and DACS, London 1992 p5t; The British-Bulgarian Friendship Society p28bl; Phil Caisley p17brt; J Allan Cash p17t; Chanel Ltd p8l; Channel Four Stills Library p9tl; Danish Tourist Board p7tl; Jane Deacon/ Angela Pollard p14, p17; European Parliament, Press and Information Office p3; Sarah Foley p5b; German Wine and Information Service p11tl, p11bl; Henry Marchant Limited Bohemian Crystal p29t; Irish Linen Guild p15; Italian State Tourist Office p16t; Lego UK Limited p7tr; Luxembourg National Tourist Tourist and Trade Office p16t; Henk Meijer, Utrecht p21l; Monaco Government Tourist and Convention Office p28t; The Morris Federation p26b; National Tourist Organisation of Greece p13; Netherlands Board of Tourism p21r; Polish Cultural Institute p29l; Portuguese National Tourist Office p23; Public Information Office, House of Commons p26t; Régie Departementale du Tourisme do la Dordogne p9tr; Rolex Watch Company Limited p29t; Silkeborg Museum p7tlb; Spanish National Tourist Office p24bl, p25; Charlotte Steedman p8br; Swedish Tourist Board p29l; Thomson Holidays p29b; Turkish Embassy Information Counsellor's Office p29r; Richard Williams p24tl.

Cover illustration by Richard Deverell.

British Library Cataloguing in Publication Data
Daly, Audrey
    The Europe project book. – (Project books)
    I. Title   II. Series
    914.0076

ISBN 0 340 56590 X

First published 1992

© 1992 Audrey Daly

Imagesetting by Litho Link Ltd., Welshpool, Powys, Wales. Printed in Hong Kong for the educational publishing division of Hodder & Stoughton Ltd, Mill Road, Dunton Green, Sevenoaks, Kent by Colorcraft Ltd.